DONEGAL TARANTELLA

Moya Cannon is an Irish poet with five published collections, the most recent being *Keats Lives* (Carcanet). The mountains, the shoreline and our primal and enduring responses to the beauty of the endangered earth are the inspiration for many of her poems. Archaeology and geology figure too as gateways to deeper understanding of our mysterious relationship with the natural world and our past.

Music, particularly traditional Irish music, has always been a deep interest and is a constant theme. She has received the Brendan Behan Award and the O'Shaughnessy Award and was 2011 Heimbold Professor of Irish Studies at Villanova University. She was born in Co. Donegal and now lives in Dublin.

DONEGAL
TARANTELLA

MOYA CANNON

CARCANET

ACKNOWLEDGEMENTS

Acknowledgements are due to the editors and publishers of *Irish Pages, Poetry Ireland Review, New Hibernia Review, PN Review, Cyphers, IASIL Journal of Irish Studies, Blood Orange Review, Japanese Journal of Irish Studies, Windharp, Connemara* and *Aran, The Strokestown Anthology, Reading the Future* and *Fermata.*

The author wishes to thank Aosdána and the Arts Council of Ireland for their continued, invaluable support.

First published in Great Britain in 2019 by
Carcanet
Alliance House, 30 Cross Street
Manchester M2 7AQ
www.carcanet.co.uk

A CIP catalogue record for this book is
available from the British Library.
ISBN 978 1 78410 787 1

Book design by Andrew Latimer
Printed in Great Britain by SRP Ltd, Exeter, Devon

The publisher acknowledges financial
assistance from Arts Council England.

CONTENTS

for Máiréad and Tim Robinson

ISLAND CORRIE

Curving back by the northern cliffs,
where a pale scar shows
that another slice of mountain
has succumbed
to this century's
hard seas
and grey storms,
we halt at a rim,
and, far below us,
in June sunlight,
blows the big, elongated O
of Lough Bunnafreva,
ringed, in this summer's long drought,
with a necklace of bleached schist.

Cupped palm of Croaghaun,
gift of a glacier,
silver doubloon of Achill.

AT THREE CASTLES HEAD WE CATCH OUR BREATH

We come from a hidden ocean and go to an unknown ocean.
– Antonio Machado

A flat, faulted slab of cliff soars
and shimmers far above us
then slants far below,
into a young ocean
we call the Atlantic.

Bedded sandstones
have been tilted on edge here –
dust of disappeared mountains,
compressed beneath the weight
of disappeared oceans.

What cosmic accident engendered
this relentless complexity of being –
the hot metal core, the mantle heavily swirling
under new hills, thin-floored oceans, fragile cities,

and under the flowering bank of earth behind us,
which responds again to the nearing of a star,
each unfolding primrose an inch of yellow velvet,
each heavy violet teetering on its slim stem,

and us, latecomers,
balanced between cliff and flowers,
trying to comprehend both,
trying to catch our breath.

FOUR HERDS OF DEER

at the back of Djouce mountain,
blent into the heather, hardly visible –
they stared at us, whistled
and sprang away,
white rumps in the air,
light, light, as deer on cave walls.

FLOWERS KNOW NOTHING OF OUR GRIEF

for Eivlin, Kieran and Patrick

The dog creeps out of her bed at night,
pads towards the bedroom door,
bumps against it as she turns to lie down,
whimpers, stays close
and licks her paw.

But the roses, pink and delicate,
unfurl their buds in the sunshine,
scent the steps up to the front door.

Their indifference should break us,
instead, they shore up a dyke
against despair;
they play a tune in a minor key;
they whisper among themselves
in an old Esperanto;
they intimate
that hope is never dead
until this bewildered earth stops
throwing up roses.

11.06.2016

MAL'TA BOY, 22,000 BC

The palaces of the tsars rise up again
newly gilded and painted, along the Neva.
Curled up in a dusty display case
in a corner of their great palace
is the rickle of a four-year-old child's bones,
found under a stone slab
by a lake in eastern Siberia.
Half of his skull painted red,
he was buried with his necklet and bracelet,
his arrowheads and swan amulet.

Small nomad, buried as your people
moved on their circuits, tracking herds
of reindeer and mammoth,
flocks of waterbirds,

a slice of your arm bone is pored over
by tribes of scientists in laboratories.
On bright screens,
they unravel the hidden
code of your genes,
shoot images around the globe
to track skeins of our human journeys
eastwards and westwards,
across three continents –
footfalls on rock, on snow, on grass
in sandy river fords.

Fallen sparrow,
improbable little kinsman,
buried with a baby sibling,

what are the filaments
that join us?
Did you pull flowers
when the snows melted?
Did you run after flapping birds?
Did you die in affliction
or in your sleep?
What did you call your mother?
For how many moons
did she weep?

THE IDIOT

Yesterday I crossed the Neva,
this morning I climbed the chipped, grubby stone stairs
to Alexander Blok's apartment, where he lived,
first in modest comfort
then, after the revolution,
where he shivered, starved and died.

This afternoon I crossed
a small park behind a street
to the apartment where Anna Akhmatova
moved in with her lover, his wife and daughter,
saw the corridor where her lover set up his darkroom,
where her student son set up home.

Three nights this week we ate
in a restaurant called 'The Idiot'.

Is there any tourist so idiotic
as one who rummages for a writer's soul
in her desk; among all the lame,
rejected, ink-and-paper tigers;
among the photos on the dining-room wall;
among the plates and pots on his kitchen shelf?

Blok's desk is as neat as a managing director's;
a writer's saucepan is only slightly
less shiny than the average,
but for that revealed inner life,
that record of yearning and survival,
which reached an arm out to save us,
in the youthful nights

when black waves crashed in,
one burying the other,
for that, we must go back
and turn page
after tattered page.

EXILE

The Shah of Iran
sent a present of an elephant
to the Tsar of Russia.

He had it delivered to a southern port
from which it was walked north
through villages where it terrified the serfs.

When it arrived in St Petersburg
it sickened, and did not live long,
although it was given vodka.

ONE OF THE MOST FOOLISH QUESTIONS

I ever asked was of a young
historian in Florida.
I asked her that Irish question,
used to keep conversation flowing,
if she knew where her family
had come from originally.

She paused and said, *It is difficult –
you can tell a certain amount from
auction sales records and cargo lists.*

But one family, she said, had a song,
which they had managed
to track back
to a village in Senegal.

BREAD

The suitcase is only half-unpacked
the washing not done,
the floor not swept,
but the oven is humming,
a sticky bowl and spoon
are in the sink
and the old alchemy of water,
flour and leaven has begun.

Soon high crusts will gild,
three loaves will be tapped
from their tins,
an aroma will flow
through keyholes,
will slip
over chipped saddle-boards,

proclaiming more eloquently
than a thrush delivering
its blue and gold aria
from the top of a telegraph pole,
than a procession
with lifted banners
and trumpets,
than a dog panting wagging circles
around a room,
Home, home, home, home!

GRAFFITI MAKES NOTHING HAPPEN

The summer before last, four girls
scraped their names in large letters,
ANGEL, CRYSTAL, KERRI + KIMI,
into the old sand cliff at Shanganagh
and beside them wrote LOVE + COMPASSION.

Above them, sand martins
swung and hunted in the moist air,
scribed the sky with nib-quick wings,
then homed into their cliffside burrows,
nurseries to a hundred fledglings.

As the girls wrote,
a milk-blue tide behind them
diligently sifted the shingle, turned
each veined pebble over again,
found it a new resting place.

The girls went home
and the martins flew down to Africa
but the cliff still beams out its blurring message,
to dogs and walkers, and to a roiling
brown, winter sea, which tosses up
rocks and plastic bottles and dead young seals.

SAND MARTINS AT SHANGANAGH

for Kevin and Bridget O Donoghue

The loves and dogged housekeeping of sand martins
undermine cliffs of clay, sand and gravel,
laid down by oceans, great rivers and glaciers.

Their burrows puncture a layer of finest sand.
Blithe sappers, they hardly care that
when they are well south of the equator,
sea gales and weeks of winter rain
might conspire to bring down
chunks of the old sand cliffs

despite the frantic scrambling
of cliff-edge briars to hold on, hold on,
the futile claims of fence posts
which dangle for months from barbed wire
before tumbling from cliff-top to shore,
or the protests of the last fragments
of a railway built to carry daytrippers,
in straw hats and starched frocks,
along a track which now crosses
spaces of the imagination.

The railway's chiselled granite blocks
are long fallen to the shingle,
corners smoothed and rounded
by a century of spring tides.

But the sand martins are indifferent
to railways and forgotten journeys.
Their tasks are old and urgent.

They have chicks to feed,
to school in a geometry of grace;
to train, on newly fledged wings,
to shoot out, up over the golf course
and the glowing buttercup fields
then down over a seaweed-draped shore
darting in twittering ellipses,
unchartable to mathematics,
as they prey on flying insects
then slip into the sandy cliff-face

until, if their frail houses last out the rain,
they have gathered enough fat and are fit,
as summer light shifts down to autumn
to fly south to Africa, to face storms
and droughts our kind may have brought on,
as their wing-feathers, reed-bones,
and ever more mysterious memories
stitch northern and southern hemispheres.

A THREE-SEAL MORNING

Yesterday's storm rearranged the shingle
onto fresh mounds and ridges

but now, the sun has laid a gold finger
on the incoming folds of the sea.

Three seals hang in the water, noses up
near a round of stones and seaweed
which could be the drowned village of Longnon.

A small wave draws its breath in
and oval pebbles at the sea's edge

lean forward, faces at a concert –
a long, clicking stone-ripple –
then, gently, fall back.

AT SHANKILL BEACH

When a wave hauls back
it leaves its gleam in saturated sand
and, sudden, up from below, the lugworms
push the darkened sand in little coils and hills.

Where are they going in the dark,
working their tiny miracle,
turning plants into animals again,
eating their way blindly
through their known world?

WINTER MORNING, THE IRISH SEA

This sea has been described as snot-green,
but, this morning, it is dishwater grey.
Waves slant in from the north,
rear up and collapse on themselves,
retreat in a rattle of sea-stones.
I think no one could love it
as the indigo Atlantic is loved

but I turn south and the sun,
a quick green dot, a red blip
starts up, flings a gold arm out across
the bay, a god of morning yawning,
and then the whole burning lid
is sitting up on the world's rim
and the sea is shaken silver silk
and white lace froths in and in and in
along the whole stony length of the shore.

RETURNS

I

May the second, and the sand martins are back with the sun.
Was there ever such excitement at a home-coming
as they dive in and out of their storm-ruined homes?
Their shadows soar and switch on the blonde sea-cliff
as the sun doubles their dance.
What joke of evolution induced birds to burrow,
like rabbits, in sand – storm petrels, shear-waters,
orange-booted puffins, sand martins –
birds who spend so long on the wing, on the sea
they can't prove title to rock, bush or tree?

II

When I was very small, there was a big family
who tumbled into school, always late, with unkempt,
pudding-bowl haircuts, always full of excuses
about missed days, undone homework and sore throats.
We knew that, most years, they arrived from Glasgow
to squat in a broken-down gatehouse. And one year
they did not come back, nor the next, nor ever.
And where are they now? They were just children like us.
Do they have grandchildren? Were they loved?
Did they know justice in the end?
Does even one of them own a safe, snug nest?

AILSA CRAIG –

for Sarah Gatley

Carraig Alasdair,
Paddy's milestone,
Ealasaid a' Chuain.
wind-skelped isle,
high, brooding ships' marker,
foam-broken parish of sea birds,
stubborn mountain core,
stepping-stone between countries,
roost for mad Sweeney,
eyrie for goats,
backdrop for golfers,

upturned pudding-bowl
of a granite,
so fine-grained
its quarried, polished
stones are sent scudding
across frozen lakes for sport.

And, as if to prove
that everything,
in the long storm of time,
can become its opposite

a cool knuckle of granite
buff-coloured and lapis-blue –
exotic as rhododendron
in a northern forest –
rumbled down the Irish sea
by long-gone glaciers

and today's tides,
gleams, this morning,
by my shoe,
betraying nothing
of a dizzy history,
a hell-hot source.

NEIGHBOUR

i.m. Harry Alcorn

The war had made a tailor of him. When he came home
he served his time with Davey Stuart. Forty years later
we would push through a hole in the hedge
and climb up onto the bench with him to hunt
for big spools among scraps of thorn-proof suiting.
My sister was there one day when his new leg arrived.

We'd share the brass-studded leather settee
with his disabled wife, waiting impatiently
for the test card to go and for *Blue Peter*
to light up on a small, brown, Bush TV,
which was everlastingly tuned to BBC,
and one day we saw him gently comb her hair.

When we were leaving, he'd reach up to a high press
and come back with a wrapped sweet each.
Working in Scotland, he'd 'listed, with a friend,
at seventeen, after another white-feather taunt.
For a year, he served at the front.
Every November, he used to lay the wreath.

When we were older and questioned him
He didn't say much, told my brother of a sergeant
who was good to him in the training camp
in Rossie, where they also taught reading.
As a boy in Horn Head, school was miles away
down a steep road and he was useful on the farm.

He mentioned *revally* and foraging, chasing
after chickens in France; places called *Arras* and *Wipers*;
You were up and down them trenches that much
you wouldn't know where you were. He'd met
Italian troops, *Tidy wee men in tidy wee uniforms.*
Now, as he took the measure of small farmers,

brought them back for unhurried fittings,
the stories of the townlands flowed in to him
as he pinned and chalked. Though discreet,
he had mastered the art of seamless speech –
he stood, talking, in the doorway on his stick
as customers reluctantly attempted retreat.

At eighty-six he fell and broke a collar bone
and was happy, at first, in the veterans' hospital
in Dublin – a party, *a wee half 'un,*
old army songs. But two months later
they'd stopped strapping on his wooden leg
and he lay in the iron bed, his flow

of slow, droll talk dried up like a summer burn
because neither nurse nor orderly knew how to turn it on.
I held his bruised-looking, blue-veined hand,
and at last heard him murmur, *I want to hear the water.*
Next day, two neighbours and my father
drove four hundred miles to bring him home.

My mother claimed it was the Lourdes water
they gave him when he passed out near Omagh
that brought him the last bit. Whatever about that papish sip,
he rallied and lived ten years more, near the shore.
We never heard what he suffered or did, as empires poured
young men's lives, like grains of sand, into Flanders mud.

He remembered that *bawn* was the French for *good*.

DONEGAL TARANTELLA

for Ronan Galvin

Tunes wash up, ocean-polished pebbles,
in the kitchens of south Donegal –
mazurkas, germans, highlands, hornpipes, jigs, reels,
all gone native since they were washed in
by waves of returning emigrants,
Napoleonic garrisons,
travelling pipers or fiddling tinsmiths.

And in one fiddling family
a tarantella was passed down
from a time before the famine,
before there was a fiddle in any house,
when shelter was afforded to a sailor,
rescued from the wreck of the *Grassen* –
out of Bergen, bound for Naples –
who, one night at a house dance,
joined in the lilting,
with a tune from his native Italy,
to please a girl or
to keep the dancers going
on a floor of beaten clay,
a new tune, a gift,
a ringing coin,
tossed into the trove
of northern music.

THE BOY WHO SWAPPED A BOG FOR A GRAMOPHONE
for Eddie O Gara

The boy, a musician already at fourteen,
walked four miles with his brother
along the Glen Road
to the fair in Carrick.

When they had seen enough
of sheep and huckster stalls,
they noticed a gramophone
and gathered up courage
to ask the shopkeeper
to play a record.

They hung about so long,
listening and wondering
that the shopkeeper, who knew
the mountainy townland
they came from – Mín na bhFachrán,
named for healing bogbine,
known for music –
proposed a barter,
the gramophone for turf-cutting rights.

The boys walked home,
taking turns to carry the gramophone
and three records.
We don't now how many cartloads of turf
the shopkeeper took out of the bog
or for how many summers

or what the boys' father,
a fiddler in a valley of fiddlers, said
or who got the better part of the bargain,
only that they had dry turf in Carrick that winter
and that a new music was played
all down the valley.

GLENCOLMCILLE SOUNDTRACK

All day long, as I climbed,
in sunshine, up to the holy well,
then on to the Napoleonic watchtower,
and halted behind it, on a headland
tramped brown by sheep,
to watch the sea carve slow blue paths
through cliffs and skerries,
May's soundtrack played on and on –
bee-hum, the high *meheh* of hill-lambs,
the lifted songs of larks in warm grass
and later, near the court tomb in the valley,
the cuckoo's shameless call.

How did we forget it,
mislay or roll it up?
– this tapestry of sound
which pleasured us
by spilling hawthorn hedges
in whin-scented summer,
as pools of yellow iris
were conjured out of wet fields
and late bluebells, vetch and fern
recaptured the ditches.

for Susan Hiller

my mother, who could not sing, told me.
As a young woman, she helped garner
the last grains of Tyrone Irish.
A teetotaller, her job
was to carry the whiskey bottle
which uncorked memory –
the old people remembered scraps of songs
when they remembered nothing else.

And today I heard a recorded lullaby
sung by a woman long dead,
in Kulkhassi, a language also dead.

No one understands the words
or knows what the singer might have sung
to an infant who may be a grandparent today
walking, haltingly, in the shade,
down a street in South Africa.

Did she sing about stars, or rain,
or tall grass, or blue flowers,
or small boats on a quick, brown river
or antelopes in a mountain valley
or a dark spirit who might snatch away
a little child.

Whatever promises or prayers
the song's words held
in that forever lost language
the mystery remains
that any infant on this hurried earth
could still feel the lullaby's intent.

Through its rhythms and syllables
love pours still
like milk
through a round sieve.

WHERE IS MUSIC STORED
for Leo and Clare

in a small corner
of the human brain,
the bird's brain,
in the subtle intelligence of water?

Or is it hoarded
in the muscles and sinews
of human hands and arms,
of a human throat,
a bird's throat,
or in the stone and silver throat,
of a mountain rivulet?

A musician recalls a tune
she hasn't played for years,
discovers it like a book on a high shelf,
a scarf slipped down the back of a wardrobe,
.

Strings, keys, are fingered tentatively,
brain cells call up mathematical patterns,
a tune starts to flow,
to find form, clear and quick,
in the vibrating air –
cadences which permit us to share
our unworded joy, yearning, despair.

THE RECORDS

have come down from the attic
to fill a low shelf.
Serious investments,
unsleeved, the needle dropped,

they were the black magic
which allowed beautiful, long-haired
America, in bell-bottomed jeans and garlands,
to stroll into our college bedsits,
to sit cross-legged and play guitar.
Simon and Garfunkle, Dylan and Joan Baez
sang through a joss-stick haze
while wax dripped from homemade candles.

We imprinted on the singer or band,
whose vibration matched our timbre,
whose songs seemed to understand,
the storm clouds in our hearts, blood, minds –
Crosby, Stills, Nash and Young, Steeleye Span,
Joni Mitchell, the bearded folk musicians,
the traditional songs and tunes
which sang through us, as though our bones knew
the music, long before a gold-tipped bow
drew it out of strings and wood, or it flowed
from the chanter, the wrist-played drones.

On the scuffed, square record sleeves
the musicians remain handsome and young;
I am not sixteen or twenty-one
and don't want to return
to the inner hurricanes

of those tossed, bewildered years.
But our records gave us rough-drawn charts
of oceans of yearning, bliss and fear,
so, warped and scratched LPs,
play on, play on, play us on.

A SENTIMENTAL EDUCATION

On the brown wireless with the dented mesh
Bing Crosby sang
Oh, my name is MacNamara,
I'm the leader of the band.
I marched up and down the brown-tiled kitchen,
as my mother washed dishes,
soaped and starched shirt collars
ironed, and we both sang tunelessly along.

Andy Stewart sang,
There was a soldier, a Scottish soldier...
Even at three or four, I felt that soldier's homesickness –
Because those green hills are no' Highland hills
They're no' island hills, they no' my land hills...
Felt, maybe, her homesickness, too,
for her green hills of Tyrone.

Elvis sang,
Can't you see that I love you?
Please don't break my heart in two.
I sang in puzzlement and she tried to explain,
Wooden heart, heart break
but how does a small child know metaphor?

Odetta sang
I know where I'm going
and I know who's going with me.
And I sang it endlessly, ecstatically,
before we went, just her and me
on the bus and train to visit her old home.

There was even a song which we sang
when she washed our hair on Saturday night
with Fairy soap and our eyes stung –
Hang down your head Tom Dooley
hang down your head and cry.
And then she towelled my hair hurriedly
combed and parted it,
and tried to encourage a quiff.

THE COUNTERMANDING ORDER, 1916

And my young grandmother,
what of her?
Was she, too, dejected?
No documentary evidence exists.
My mother, too young, at seven months,
to remember, herself, used tell us,
She heard the horse and trap in the yard again
and could not believe her ears.

What was my grandmother doing?
Did she clear away a half-eaten Easter dinner
talking, distractedly, to her two little boys,
as she scraped jelly from a glass bowl?
Did she mix feed for hens or pigs,
or wonder about bringing cattle in for milking?
Did she pray, or take out her handwork?
Was she putting the baby down for her rest?

Only hours earlier, in the swept farmyard,
she had said goodbye to her husband of six years,
her exiled lover of seven more,
whose letters had been carried in steamships
across Caribbean and Atlantic tides.

On this Sunday morning, had they embraced
as he headed for the muster at Dungannon?
– as he enjoined her to bring up the children
as *good Catholics and good Irishmen and Irishwomen.*
(My mother, in old age, was to remark, with a raised eyebrow,
Wasn't it cool of him, all the same?)

Now, as the trap clattered in through the gate
and the horse, Rebel, halted in his familiar place,
did my young grandmother wipe her hands on her apron,
did she rush to the door?

Although the rising had been called off,
although the great cause seemed lost again,
did her heart not rejoice?

OCTOBER 1945

It was two months later
two months after a small sun
opened its belly over the city
and pressed Hiroshima into the ground.

After two months of trudging
and turning rubble she found it
under a melted bottle – her daughter's
scorched wooden sandal,
There was no mistaking the straps
she had made from her old kimono.

HARD LESSONS

Five hundred Hiroshima schoolgirls
and their teachers
had been pulling down

wooden houses,
removing clay tiles.
to create a fire-break
for fear of bombing raids.

The sculptor gives us three of them,
three thirteen-year-olds
two with plaits, one with bobbed hair,
holding a box marked with $E=mc^2$.

Beside the loveliest building in the world,
a white flower on a silk-blue sky,
between the ribbed arches of the women's pavilion,
bees have swarmed.
Their hive is a brown blob
in the rose-coloured roof.
The bees hardly notice the awed, exhausted crowds
draped in multi-coloured silk, cotton and nylon
who press far below them each day.
They may not even notice
the white palace built for a dead wife.

By the long narrow ponds
they plunder the flowers –
pink and blue forget-me-nots;
they dodge the white, long-limbed egrets
who high-step among the blossoms.
The bees neither know nor care
that the beloved queen, the favoured wife,
died near a battlefield,
having birthed her fourteenth child,
or that, to build the floating dome,
white marble slabs were balanced
on the backs of elephants and hauled,
for three and a quarter miles,
up a spiral wooden ramp
which was dismantled in a night.

The bees have their own work to do.
They have a hive to build,
a queen to serve,
larvae to feed,
honey to make.

ST PATRICK'S WELL, ORVIETO
(Pozzo di San Patrizio, Orvieto)

    for Eiléan and Macdara

When Pope Clement VII took refuge
in the high, walled city
while Rome was being sacked,
by the Holy Roman Emperor,

he feared a siege,
so had the master architect,
Antonio da Sangallo the Younger,
cut a well fifty metres

down through bedrock,
a well much deeper even, and wider
than the Etruscan well of Perugia,
almost as deep

as Saladin's well at Cairo.
Seventy internal windows
lit its two graceful staircases
which intertwined in a double helix,

so one mule could descend
the broad steps
while another toiled up
with barrels of water,

a well so deep
it almost touched Purgatory.

THE COIMBRA LIBRARIANS

In the Biblioteca Joanina –
a gilt, rococo palace for leather-bound books –
the most beautiful and precious volumes
are laid open in display cases.
Each evening, before turning out the lights,
crossing the inlaid, marble floor
and softly closing, then locking,
a small door cut out of the great door,
the librarian drapes the cases

in sheets of hide, to protect them
against dirt dropped
by the library's night guardians –

a colony of small bats
who flit between soaring oak bookcases,
who skim
                    between geography
                            and astronomy,
            who zig-zag,
blindly,
            between science,
                    history,
            and the lives of saints,
who dart past
            the volumes
                    of the Procedural Records
            of the Inquisition,
all the dark night,
                    swooping
                            on bookworms.

SPOONS
  for Marie Foley

Sometimes we write out of darkness,
sometimes out of cool morning light,
sometimes the bird-feeder is empty,
sometimes there are five goldfinches.

Who carved the first spoon?
I don't mean a seashell
or a scoop of wood.
I mean a long-handled bone spoon
which fitted into a baby's mouth
like these in the Valencia museum,
spoons six thousand years old,
discovered in the Cova de l'Or.

When did we learn to give?
First it was kisses, then milk,
then someone invented the spoon.

CORRIB

for Eva Bourke

This river drew me to live here –
its dragon-energy after a storm
as black water from the lake
leapt in standing waves at night
between high limestone walls
or surged, light-lanced in the morning –
a tumult of white under bridges.

Its foam-falling weirs are pitched
at the angle of desire;
its canals flow alongside,
then curve off,
towards some lost or broken mill-race.

I should not love it.
I have seen search boats
and firemen clustered at the last lock
and fresh bouquets cello-taped
to quayside railings
with cellophane-wrapped tributes
to *the best brother in the world…*

Since I came here
this river has seduced
so many despairing
young women and men,
who were blind as Cupid
to their own beauty,
to the loves which failed to hold them.

Yet, on a June day,
the high-shouldered heron
guards the Fishery Tower;
mullet hang thickly under the last bridge
the lit estuary brims
with swans and cormorants;
the seal swims strongly in;
the Arctic tern punctures the tide
and the river opens out to the Atlantic
like possibility itself, or a very old song.

NO PULSE

And my old home has been dismantled –
books and CDs have been pruned and boxed,
never-used soup plates and sherry glasses
returned to the charity shop,
half the furniture passed on
to friends or young relatives
and pictures shrouded in bubble-wrap.

Pink cabbage roses,
which rooted long before I did,
three decades ago,

rub against
the kitchen window,
like an old cat.

In the white-painted yard
bins are crammed to the brim;

the emptied house gleams –
a freshly washed glass –

and I drift above it in mild surprise –
a crab, who has hauled herself out
of an old carapace,
who strains to hear
departed music.

AT DOG'S BAY

This winter's storms have chewed off
half a row of dunes
have revealed a line of midden –
a charcoal stroke across a page of clean time
burnt winkles, burnt bones, burnt wood –
hearths smoored forever by the tail-swish
of some pre-historic hurricane.

And above the midden line,
in the fresh sand-cliff,
is a crooked line of burrows –
a new city,
a twittering, cliffside pueblo,
a lively Petra,
where sand martins,
rested after their Sahara crossing,
are swallowed up and shot out
to brush the sky
with quick calligraphy,
jubilant diagonals.

IN DERRYCLARE WOODS

Sleeved in green velvet
and violets, an oak limb
thrown over the stream.

THE RING-FORTS

The scalpel-cut of the new motorway
brings them closer to our speeding minds,
so full of codes, contacts and pin numbers.

How discreet these earth rings are
how quiet, with their sloped green banks
their muddy, cattle-trod entries,
their enclosures of briars and nettles
and, often, their cool souterraines,
their groves of trees,
their Norman keeps.

The April fields hold so many of them
as though some old god had gone crazy
with a round stamp or a giant pastry-cutter.

Apart from a mention in the annals,
a cadence of a song, a shred of a story,
we don't know much of what went on
in this or that *cathair*, *dún* or *lios*,
only that they are all done with war
and trouble, with love and music.
How completely erased
are the ordinary, busy lives lived
within these green circles.

Once, through a haze of illness,
I was unaccountably gladdened
driving past a snapping line of white washing
strung right across a ring-fort,
line ends lashed to two sycamores.

DEFENCE SYSTEM

Those round, squat, granite towers
were built around the coast
at immense cost
to keep Napoleon out.

He never came, and not one shot
was fired from them
at a French ship, until lately
and then, only as a salute.

Their fame derives mainly now
from the jocose account,
by a young writer,
of his friend's morning shave.

FROM THE PLANE

There is a nest of gold in the cloud
And, far below, under the Atlantic,
lie the unquiet volcanoes
as the earth rips itself open
very slowly, to stretch the ocean.

Below us flows an endless white cloudfield
with occasional holes like tiny lavender lakes
like the brown, blue and silver bog lakes
in the half-drowned edges
of Connemara and Labrador
which have almost forgotten
the volcanoes that blew them apart.

FROM ABOVE THE ENGLISH CHANNEL
for Rachel Brown

Every cloud, even the smallest tuft,
drags its own shadow behind it,
on the skin of a silver-blue sea.

Foam-followed ships are white tadpoles.
They have forsaken, and seek out,
the primal embrace of harbours.

Families of nomads crossed here
before a great inundation,
which parted land masses.

Who witnessed its beginning,
as weather grew warmer,
and growth came earlier,

as tides rose a little higher,
and land at the tide's edge
vanished for the first time?

STARRY, STARRY NIGHT IN THE NATIONAL LIBRARY

Vincent, you would have loved it,
as Don McClean's song poured out
of the bottom left-hand corner of the reading room
of the Irish National Library,
loudly enough for all twenty-three readers,
drowsy browsers, graduate students,
academics on sabbatical,
to lift and turn startled heads –
sea-birds grazing a salt-marsh.

He sang for a whole yellow minute, maybe two,
while readers continued to shift and turn around
not quite upset that their silence had been stolen.

From her curved counter a librarian scanned the desks
and a brown-jacketed, middle-aged man tiptoed
from the catalogue section and gently
closed the lid of a Mac Air, and a long, slow
sigh came from all forty-four cherubs
who had been swinging their plump garlands
high on the green library wall since your time

and I was blown back to a bedsit on South Circular Road
where, forty years ago, I blu-tacked the poster
of your blue and yellow field of stars
at the head of my single bed, not finding it strange
that the stars should swirl like small suns in the pit of night,
not knowing it was painted a year before
you took your own aching, luminous life,

and you, not knowing, as you fought your darkness
and frenziedly harvested the light of stars and sickle moon,
how it would be poured into a song,
how your brush would flood a library across the sea,
a century later, with golden, starry light.

RELATIVITY — THE IVEAGH GARDENS, FORTY-FIVE YEARS LATER

I used to sit here in May sunshine,
a trespasser, at sixteen, studying for an exam,
trying to concentrate on a book
about the origins of the Second World War.

The university garden was a neglected demesne
of tumbled statues in the undergrowth
and silent fountains. The war had ended
long ago, well before I was born.

The holly trees must have been overgrown then.
There must have been wrens in the bushes, as today
but I do not remember them.
My life was in the future tense, after the exam.

I sat on a bench somewhere here
near this statue of Diana the Huntress
who has lost her head, her hands, her bow
and her arrows, all but for one feather.

The span of years arrowing back to that May
is far greater than from then to the end
of the Second World War
but it feels like no time at all.

POST-BOX IN WALL AT ROSBRIN

for Una and Con

Its mouth overflows with blossoms and starry leaves: –
it has had enough of good news and bad,
of memoriam cards, boxes of wedding cake,
birthday cards, air-letters, love letters,
postal orders, ten-shilling notes, letters
to the Co. Council, the Solicitor, the Editor.

A shower of pink, ivy-leafed toadflax has colonised it,
hiding the symbol of the queen or king,
Free State or Republican government,
who authorised its installation here,
in a freshly plastered wall,
now blurred with yellow lichen,
a stone's throw from where the road
wraps itself around a ring-fort.

There is no method of calculating
what weight of heartbreak and passion,
of joy and gossip, it has swallowed
during the decades in which
its small iron torso held in trust
the myriad privacies of a town land.

Long retired, its traffic passed on
to laptops which post news instantly,
casually, some alchemy has caused
all the near-archaic endearments
to rise to the top, to brim from its mouth
in a cascade of tiny, pink flowers –

Dear Sir, Dear Minnie,
My Dear Patrick,
A Stóirín, Dearest John,
My Darling, Dear Daddy,
faithfully, sincerely, fondly,
affectionately, yours,
ever, ever yours.

ANOTHER GREAT MAN DOWN

Zane Grey in the Davenport Hotel, Spokane, Washington

Wyoming, The Shepherd of Guadeloupe, Under the Tonto Rim,
my big brothers' outgrown cowboy books.
I wore out the romantic sections, fell in love
with all those courageous rough diamonds,
riding up atop the Mesa, or down deep canyons,
rounding up ornery steers for honest ranchers,
cooking beans and sourdough pancakes out on the range,
arriving home to their bunkhouses in need of shut-eye,
yet ever ready to leap up to quench fires in flaming barns,
or rescue hosses or steers from doggone rustlers.
Respectful, even shy with women,
they always got the purty gal in the end.

As swirling desert dust, tumbleweed and jingling spurs
cancelled out slanting rain, gaberdine coats and October Devotions,
I never expected, fifty years later, to cross paths with Zane Grey.
He was here too, in the 1920s grandeur of the Davenport.
After a luncheon with the Chamber of Commerce
he wrote about the honest ranchers who met here
to craft a plan to break a strike of seasonal workers,
of Wobblies, riff-raff, trouble-makers, itinerant harvest workers,
arriving from the east on trains, among them maybe even
some of my own distant kin, hoping for work,
a living wage, on the round-hilled wheat fields of Washington.

And I took you for one of the good guys, Zane Grey!

AT DUSK

Last night, the fox padded along
our red-brick street
under yellow fan-lights;

last week an otter,
curved and sleek as a cat
slipped across the pier in the half-light
and went down into the sea,
leaving quick prints on stone steps;

last month we saw a wild boar
and her three young
cross a road before dark
and vanish into the briars.

Her path was a track of mud
straight down a field
from the mountain forest
as it had been, months earlier,
a line of hoof-marks in snow
and, earlier still,
a crease in summer grass.

The creatures of dusk,
whom we have almost dispossessed,
continue to cross our paths,
continue to bless us.

CLOWANSTOWN FISH TRAPS, 5,000 BC

National Museum of Ireland

I must gather my traps,
she said it so often, gathering up
handbag, headscarf, string shopping bag –
I never thought to ask what kind of traps –
mouse traps, rabbit snares, badger traps?
or did the phrase come from eel-fishers,
who wove branches into tricksy cones.

Three millennia before blocks of stone
were hauled to build the Pyramids,
branches of birch, alder and rosewood
were cut, twisted into four long cones,
wedged or staked in a weir or narrow stream,
and one day, left ungathered.

They were hardly forgotten,
like a mobile phone or keys.
Some interruption – illness, death,
the season's push to move on,
or an enemy raid, a wrecking storm,
swept four traps into this glass case.

And, still, after St Patrick's Day,
when Arctic terns fly back
from South Africa to fall, white darts,
on sand-smelts in a Connemara lagoon,
a man will walk by a small stream
and wedge or stake conical fish traps.

GOLD

for Fionnuala and Reva-Ann

A century ago today
my grandmother held on
to the rods of an iron bedstead
as she pushed her first daughter
out into autumn light
which shafted
between the drawn curtains
of a northern farmhouse window.

Maureen's hair, she said,
is the colour of a new sovereign.

9/9/2015

Rose Cannon 1920 – 2016

Yesterday I saw my little, blue-eyed aunt,
still lovely after almost a century,
go, so quietly, so willingly, into the good night,
or the good light, she might already
have been aboard a reed boat,
afloat on a morning river.

Fill up the room, she had told her friend,
and in that sun-filled room,
with her big, mechanised chair,
her stuffed bookcase, and little else,
her friends came and went all day.
They held her hands, stroked her forehead,
chatted softly, and, at the end,
said prayers she had learned
as a small girl in Donegal.

When I put my hand on her arm
I felt only bone.
Over the last months
she had become a reed herself
and spoke the word 'love' more often,
with less embarrassment,
than anyone I have known.

THE TWELVE BENS...
for Lynn

yesterday morning, striding
in their shawls of rain and, later,
sun-blasted, and today
dappled under running clouds.

I start to understand why we love them,
not just their hard grey,
white and blue beauty
but also their companionability

as they pose together
in a semicircle behind the lake,
a group of friends,
arms around each others' shoulders,

as we did yesterday
smiling at the camera,
remembering our late, great friend
who loved the Glencoaghan horseshoe;

loved to name the mountains,
Derryclare, Ben Lettery, Bengowar;
who gathered us together yesterday
between mountains and estuary,

in a blue and white house
with seven welcoming doors.

THE SONG OF THE BOOKS

(AMHRÁN NA LEABHAR)

for Seamus and Bronagh

It's the plummeting second note
that knells his despair
two centuries later –
his clothes and all
his leather-bound books
drifted down among the kelp
off Derrynane –
his own poems,
his rare manuscripts in Irish,
blurring underwater,
turning to pulp
among crabs and mackerel
and the poet-schoolmaster,
who had travelled overland,
getting word
by the shore in Port McGee,
and making a song
out of utter loss.

It was not the library of Alexandria
whose shelved scrolls stored
the known world's wisdom
and claimed to cure souls,
or the library of Nineveh
or of Babylon,
where kings had imprinted
their triumphs on wet clay,

yet the bell-voiced singers
and the uilleann pipers tell it
as though the wooden sailing boat
with its small, treasured library,
identity papers of the dispossessed,
had hit that sea-hid rock,
had gone down
only yesterday.

CLIMB

A worn quartzite cone,
the mountain sails on
in and out of mist.
Below, a hundred islands come and go –
doors of perception blow open, blow closed.

NOTES

p.37, THE COUNTERMANDING ORDER: The Countermanding
Order was an order issued by Eoin MacNeill, Commander-in-Chief
of the Irish Volunteers, and published in the Sunday Independent,
Dublin, on Easter Sunday 1916. Its aim was to prevent the
countrywide uprising planned by a secret military committee drawn
from the Irish Volunteers and Irish Citizen Army, including Patrick
Pearse, Thomas Clarke, Thomas McDonagh and James Connolly.

p.51, THE RING-FORTS: *cathair, dún, lios,* Gaelic terms for ring-
forts.

p.58, POST-BOX IN WALL AT ROSBRIN: *a stóirín,* Gaelic, 'my
little treasure'.

p.66, THE SONG OF THE BOOKS: *Amhrán na Leabhar* was written
by the poet-schoolmaster, Tomás Rua Ó Súilleabháin (1785–1848).
He had been transferred from Derrynane, near the southern tip of
the Iveragh Peninsula in Co. Kerry, to Port McGee, twenty-five
miles further north. The boat on which his precious books and his
other belongings were being transported sank shortly after leaving
Derrynane. It is possible that the very beautiful melody predated the
song and may have been a harping air.